Date Due

THE DRAMA OF
THE PASSION

ARMAND GODOY

THE DRAMA
OF
THE PASSION

ENGLISH METRICAL VERSION

BY

MALCOLM McLAREN

842.9
G54d Em

29150

TO
MY SON
JEAN-CHARLES

DRAMATIS PERSONAE

JESUS
MARY
MARY MAGDALENE
THE EVANGELIST
THE DISCIPLES
THE THREE KINGS
THE WOMAN OF SAMARIA
PETER
JUDAS
PILATE
CAIAPHAS
THE PHARISEES
THE DEAD
THE NIGHT
THE NIGHTINGALE
THE LARK

A BLIND MAN
THE LIGHTNING
THE THUNDERBOLT
A BEGGAR
THE MOUNTAIN
A LEPER
THE FOREST
THE FLOWERS
THE SEA
THE PAST
THE FUTURE
CHORUS OF YOUNG MAIDENS
SATAN
DEATH
A LITTLE CHILD
FIRST SERVANT
SECOND SERVANT

VOICES, CHORUSES, GRAND CHORUS

PREFACE

THIS is, I believe, the first attempt to translate into an English metrical version the Franco-Cuban poet Armand Godoy's *Le Drame de la Passion*. (A Spanish and an Italian version have already been published ; a German one is to appear immediately.) My justification of the attempt is to make known the beauty and originality of M. Godoy's treatment of his subject—a combination of classic and romantic art.

There will always be two schools of opinion about the value of translations. Firstly those who, in the words of Albert Samain,[1] ' have a poetic horror of verse-translations. I can think of no worse labour in the world than that of painfully dismembering a thought that is already complete and finished, in order to spread it out on the Procustean bed of versification. The very *raison d'être* of poetry, that is to say its inventiveness, its feverish moments of intuition, the divine intemperance of its imagery, is lost, suppressed, and destroyed. What remains is the labour of a game of patience, which, if it is to be done conscientiously, is enough to render you insane. I said " conscientiously " ; therein lies the kernel of the problem ; the choice must be made : either your text, or that of the original.'

Secondly those who look upon translations as a means of attaining to a more mutual understanding between nations through the world diffusion of thought.

There are likewise two schools of translation : the one subjective, which is, *ipso facto*, obliged to masquerade under the guise of an adaptation rather

[1] *Des Lettres*, Albert Samain. Mercure de France, 1933.

than a translation ; the other objective, intent on vowing fidelity to the structure as well as to the spirit of the original.

The present translation unashamedly belongs to the second category.

To attempt to translate into English verse the complex harmony and the orchestral rhythm of M. Armand Godoy's masterpiece may well border on the height of folly ; and to do so, in the main, at the expense of rhyme, may be deemed to be folly itself. But—*que faire ?* Betray the original and substitute an alien image, a shallow paraphrase, in place of the ' divine intemperance ' of the original—all for the sake of a rhyme ?—*que non pas!*

The rhythm and measure of the almost symphonic progression of M. Godoy's drama being of so much more vital importance, I have preferred to labour at the feet of Rhythm—how inadequately is only too apparent!—rather than at the feet of Rhyme.

In this ungracious task I would ask M. Godoy to see a proof of the admiration I feel for this Catholic poet—mystic and ' musicist '—whose work increasingly finds its inspiration in those Joys and Sorrows which are the complementary ministers of Beauty throughout the Universe, and whose philosophy has come to rest on the serene example of that Life which culminated in the Sacrifice of the Cross.

*   *   *

For a special study of M. Godoy's poetical works, see the translator's article ' Hommage au Grand Poète Armand Godoy ' in *Modern Languages*, October 1929 (A. & C. Black).

MALCOLM McLAREN

BURFORD
  OXFORD

PART I

CHORUS

Tremble, you cold-hearted men, you widows, orphans, cursèd race!
Tremble, Kings and Beggars, Weak and Strong, you Cut-throats and your Victims!
Girt with lightning, leaning o'er us, the chastening God meditates
And seeks a torment terrible enough to punish all our crimes.

Tremble, cowardly brows and stinking bodies! Tremble, Hypocrites,
—Salt of impure kisses 'neath the flatness of unleavened bread—
For the Lamb of God who feels the Cross less heavy than our rites,
Drags in vain both Love and Pardon toward the hill's disastrous head.

As for Him, He's going to die! There'll be no more kind deeds, or tender
Words that pour upon our burning wounds the music of His power.
Scarcely will the distant, far too distant echo of the parables

Brand our sins with an uncertain odour of apples that are sour.
As for Him, He's going to die! No more Samaritans, sweet spell
That distils the Azure in the cooling fountain and the well.

15

THE EVANGELIST

When Jesus had finished these sayings, to His disciples thus He spake :

JESUS

Brethren, the feast of Passover takes place in two days.   Much distress
Already troubles Me.   'Tis by yourselves that I shall be denounced,
Beset by blasphemies, frenzied with gall, and nailed upon the Cross.

A VOICE

Jesus, well-beloved,
Say, what hast Thou done ?
Do these grieving folk
Know that they are grieved ?

Do they know Thine eyes
Hide within them flames
That purify the skies
And liberate the soul ?

Jesus, well-beloved,
Thy crime, is it mine ?
Does my grieving heart
Know it grieveth Thine ?

Does it know that Love
Curbs the bounds of Space—
Space that leadens Day,
Deepening Night above ?

Jesus, well-beloved,
Loving is Thy crime.
. I am full of grief !
Thy Love grieveth mine !

HE EVANGELIST

The chief priests and the elders came into the palace of the High Priest.
By subtlety and with a traitor's help they preconceived His death.
The hour being unpropitious :

THE PHARISEES

Keep our plan in secrecy, they said ;
Among the people the Master might provoke an uproar at the feast.

HE EVANGELIST

When Jesus had sat down to share a meal with Simon, lo ! there came
A humble woman, in her hand a lovely alabaster vase.
Upon the head divine she gently poured some perfume from the vase
While the disciples cried aloud with indignation—to their shame :

THE DISCIPLES

This is a useless offering and costly and we are but poor.
It's all a waste.   Far better had you kept this money for the poor.

THE EVANGELIST

When Jesus heard their condemnation, He was moved and said :

JESUS

This woman

Did a kindly action pouring all this perfume on my soul,
Hard-hearted men, you will not always have your Master here, you know.
Beggars, forsooth, you shall have day and night, and this I promise you
That She, this woman, shall be the standard-bearer of the gospel news :
And when the Angels come to preach the news, there they shall be with Her.

A VOICE

My whole body breathes narcissus perfume and carnation,
In my golden hair there blooms the message of the rose,
My two eyes perfume all disrespect and tribulation ;
With my breathing I embalm the abysmal sighs of Cause.

Cool, my tears are cool and fresh as any mountain spring ;
Warm and genial are my kisses like a dove's soft wing ;
More sonorous is my voice than echoes following me,
Echoes of a voice lost in the labyrinth of the tombs.

To anoint Thy forehead I remember all the passion
That I learned so long ago in the far distant South
Where the women carry in the lewdness of their mouth
The salt of ocean and the sweetness of the spring.

Tear my body!   Munch carnation and narcissus bloom!
Breathe my hair e'en though Thou crush the roses and their message!
Tell me, too, about the anguish and delight of torture,
Odious Effect that makes Cause tremble with dark gloom.

ANOTHER VOICE

Body—narcissi, carnation ;—
Hair—and bloom of rose ;—
Scent of tribulation
And murmur of Cause.

Upon the mountain, plaints—
Kisses of the doves,
And the voice that haunts
Me amongst the tombs ;

Every new caress
Learned in distant lands,
Lips lewd with excess
—Seas, and all the springs. . . .

'Tis for Thee the mountain,
'Tis for Thee the doves,
'Tis for Thee the friend
Searching in the tombs ;

For Thee each caress
Learned in distant lands,
Springs flush with excess :
Seas, and watery wastes.

For Thee the carnations,
Narcissi and rose,
For me all the tribulations—
Both Effect and Cause.

THE EVANGELIST

Then one of them went unto the chief priest
And said :

JUDAS

I will deliver you my Master.
What will you give me ?

THE EVANGELIST

And they gave in silver
Thirty pieces, and when the pact was sealed
The cursed apostle waited for his Victim,
Seeking a chance to carry out his crime.

A VOICE

O kisses, all the kisses of my childhood
With honey and with silver light imbued,
O come, O come, O come to my defence!
—My lips already taste the bitter cup.

O kisses of my love, whose song perhaps
Like Will o' the wisps dances among the tombs,
O quickly fill me with your cadences!
—I hear the cruel viper's strident hiss.

Kisses supreme given to a body without shame,
Ah! give me now, give me your mystic flame
To calcinate my fratricidal mouth

Before it hide beneath your charming youth
That poison which shall cause the tears to flow,
All, all the tears of the abortive earth!

THE EVANGELIST

*Now the Apostles on the first day of the feast of unleavened bread
Said to the Master :*

THE DISCIPLES

Where wilt Thou that we prepare Thee the Passover ?

THE EVANGELIST

To which He answered :

JESUS

In the town, go find the man who's one of us,
And say to him : 'The hour is come.   He wants to celebrate Passover
With us at your house.'

THE EVANGELIST

Now when they were sat down
He said :

JESUS

Listen to me!
Here is in very truth
The ignoble treachery :
Betrayed by one of you,
They'll cast me into prison
And I shall bear the Cross.

THE EVANGELIST

They all cried :

THE DISCIPLES

One of us!
And is it I ?   Or I ?

23

CHORUS

O kisses, all the kisses of my childhood
With honey and with silver light imbued,
O come, O come, O come to my defence!
—My lips already taste the bitter cup.

O kisses of my love, whose song perhaps
Like Will o' the wisps dances among the tombs,
O quickly fill me with your cadences!
—I hear the cruel viper's strident hiss.

Kisses supreme given to a body without shame,
Ah! give me now, give me your mystic flame
To calcinate my fratricidal mouth

Before it hide beneath your charming youth
That poison which shall cause the tears to flow,
All, all the tears of the abortive earth!

THE EVANGELIST

Jesus said :

JESUS

'Tis he that dippeth with Me in the dish, yea he
Shall betray your Lord and Master.   Know that I shall be condemned.

It is written I shall go away.   But woe unto that man
Who doth betray Me.   Better far for him that he had not been born.

THE EVANGELIST

Now Judas who betrayed
Arose and spake and said:

JUDAS

O Master, is it I?

THE EVANGELIST

Jesus said unto him:

JESUS

Thou hast said.

A VOICE

O kisses, all the kisses of my childhood
With honey and with silver light imbued,
O come, O come, O come to my defence!
—My lips already taste the bitter cup.

O kisses of my love, whose song perhaps
Like Will o' the wisps dances among the tombs,
O quickly fill me with your cadences!
—I hear the cruel viper's strident hiss.

Kisses supreme given to a body without shame,
Ah ! give me now, give me your mystic flame
To calcinate my fratricidal mouth

Before it hide beneath your charming youth
That poison which shall cause the tears to flow,
All, all the tears of the abortive earth!

THE EVANGELIST

*Then, while they were at supper, Jesus took some bread and blessing it,
He brake it, giving it to His disciples as He said to them :*

JESUS

Take this and eat!   This is My Body!

THE EVANGELIST

Then He said, raising His cup :

26

JESUS

This is My Blood! Drink, all of you! This is the last time I shall drink,
Until I drink with you when I shall reach the Kingdom of My Father!

A VOICE

Well of love—Thy body is as white as purest snow,
As rhythmic as flowing waters dying on the shore,
Fragrant too as myrrh, as soft as down on peaches ripe,
Candid like the lily and blythe as soarings of a Dream.

Balm, Thy body, balm of nightmare and of violence,
Veil that covers our remorse,—and sweetest hour of armistice,—
Star that pours upon the burning ardours of our wounds,
Like a sparkling ocean wave, its long and brief caress.

Master mine, Thy body is as white as purest snow.
Balm, Thy body, balm of nightmare and of violence.

ANOTHER VOICE

Crimson flows Thy blood and tints the sunset and the cherries
And the brow of maidens and the hands and small pink feet
Of all tiny children and the windows of our churches
And the hardy petals of the wild-grown oleander.

Crimson flows Thy blood, elixir which impassions us
So that we may plant our roses on the topmost rocks,
Finding in the height of any tempest those warm breezes
Which can deck with butterflies the pit of every Cause.

Crimson flows Thy blood and tints the sunset and the cherries,
The flesh of tiny children and the windows of our churches.

THE EVANGELIST

*Then when they'd sung the Paschal hymn, with one accord they all went out
Unto the Mount of Olives.   And Jesus spake unto them, saying :*

JESUS

I shall offend you all and be the cause of your decline and fall,
For it is written :
' I will smite the Shepherd and the sheep of the flock shall be scattered abroad
But after,
When I shall come to life again, 'tis I shall go before you all
In Galilee.

CHORUS

The sheep shall go and wander through a foreign land
And yet shall seek in vain, alas! the Shepherd's track

Both day and night, nor sleep, nor drink, nor any food,
The sheep, alas! shall seek in vain the Shepherd's track.

The sheep, O Shepherd, they shall bleat with painfulness,
The burden of Remorse lie lightly on their back.

The sheep shall seek in every orchard, every cave,
Yet all in vain, they shall not find the Shepherd's track.

But one day He shall come, the Messenger divine,
And in His arms He'll bring the flowers of orange-trees.

The sheep shall sniff the blossoms of the orange-trees ;
With love, O Shepherd, bleating love they'll fill the leas.

A VOICE

Browse, sheep, O browse the foliage of the orange-trees,
The Shepherd's Star is surely watching o'er the leas.

HE EVANGELIST

Now Peter in reply to Jesus said :

PETER

O Master, even if
All men should be offended at Thy sight, I'll ne'er deny Thee, Lord.

THE EVANGELIST

Jesus replying said :

JESUS

I tell thee, verily, that even this night,
Peter, before the cock shall crow, thou surely shalt deny Me thrice.

THE EVANGELIST

Peter replied :

PETER

No never!   Even if, so be, I die with Thee.

THE EVANGELIST

Every disciple also gave his word in the same way,
And Jesus went unto a place called Gethsemane
With them and said :

JESUS

Now sit ye here,
Whilst I depart awhile to pray.

THE EVANGELIST

With Him He took Peter and the two sons of Zebedee,
And feeling very sorrowful and heavy said to them :

JESUS

My soul is sad even unto death.
   Stay here with Me!
   And watch with Me!

A VOICE

My soul is sad even unto death.
A thousand vipers rob my breath.
Indifferent, the whole earth sleeps.
The golden-voiced lovers dream
Of their delight, of their remorse,
And greedy man tells out his gold.
My soul is sad even unto death.

The stags give ear—again, again!—
To the portentous bugle call ;
The sea pulsates as it retreats,
The ocean breeze becomes so strong
That dove with condor fly abreast.
My soul is sad even unto death.

Indifferent, the whole earth sleeps,
And like a treasure I collect
The echoes of the golden voice.
They follow me—again, again!
More unrelenting than Remorse.
My body shrinks to shun itself.
My soul is sad even unto death.

CHORUS

Over Thy body and Thy soul be lord,
Thy Father holds the true reward.

A VOICE

My soul is sad even unto death.

CHORUS

Quietens the sea, the wind's no breath,
Beneath Thy feet is groaning Death.

A VOICE

The golden-voiced lovers dream.

CHORUS

Flee from Delight, flee from Remorse!

A VOICE

Lo! dove and condor fly abreast.

CHORUS

List to the azure's golden breath!

A VOICE

My soul is sad even unto death.

THE EVANGELIST

Then, when He'd gone a little further, He fell upon His face and prayed:

JESUS

O Father, if it be but possible, let this cup pass from Me!
Yet, Father, let
Thy will be done!

THE EVANGELIST

And coming back to His disciples fast asleep, He said to Peter :

JESUS

How now ?   And was one hour alone too long for you to watch with Me ?
To flee temptation, watch and pray : the spirit wills, the flesh is weak.

THE EVANGELIST

A second time
He went away
And thus He prayed :

JESUS

If this cup may not
Pass away from Me,
          Thy will be done.

A VOICE

Hast Thou remembrance of Thy childhood's hours,
The song of trees, the radiance of the flowers,
Thy mother's soft embrace insatiate
That made the sounds and colours palpitate ?

The valley's deepness dost Thou recognize
Where used to plunge Thy great clairvoyant eyes
Laden with kindness and encouragement
To soothe all suffering and embarrassment ?

Hast Thou remembrance of that maiden's art
Whose body was perfumed with heliotrope
Arrested by Thine eyes beside the well,

Whose moistened lips importunate with hope
Nearly submerged Thine awe-inspiring heart
In the Lethan waters' magic spell ?

THE EVANGELIST

He came back and found them all once more asleep,
For their eyes were heavy with unwonted vigil.
Leaving them He drew aside and prayed the same.
Then to His disciples cometh He again :

JESUS

You may sleep now
And rest awhile! . . .

The hour is nigh,
The Son of Man
Is in the hands
Of sinners.   Rise
And let us go!
He that betrays
Me is at hand.

A VOICE

O kisses, all the kisses of my childhood
With honey and with silver light imbued,
O come, O come, O come to my defence!
—My lips already taste the bitter cup.

O kisses of my love, whose song perhaps
Like Will o' the wisps dances among the tombs,
O quickly fill me with your cadences!
—I hear the cruel viper's strident hiss.

Kisses supreme given to a body without shame,
Ah! give me now, give me your mystic flame
To calcinate my fratricidal mouth

Before it hide beneath your charming youth
That poison which shall cause the tears to flow,
All, all the tears of the abortive earth!

THE EVANGELIST

And while He was yet speaking
Judas, one of the Twelve,
Came forth accompanied
By a great multitude
Armed with swords and staves
By order of the priests
And the elders of the people.
He that betrayed Him
Gave unto them a sign :
'Whomever I shall kiss,
That same is He.   Hold Him !'
And coming up to Jesus
He said to Him :

JUDAS

Hail, Master !

CHORUS

O kisses, all the kisses of my childhood
With honey and with silver light imbued,

O come, O come, O come to my defence!
—My lips already taste the bitter cup.

O kisses of my love, whose song perhaps
Like Will o' the wisps dances among the tombs,
O quickly fill me with your cadences!
—I hear the cruel viper's strident hiss.

Kisses supreme given to a body without shame,
Ah! give me now, give me your mystic flame
To calcinate my fratricidal mouth

Before it hide beneath your charming youth
That poison which shall cause the tears to flow,
All, all the tears of the abortive earth!

THE EVANGELIST

He kissed Him.
Jesus said :

JESUS

Friend,
Wherefore art thou come ?

THE EVANGELIST

Then they that were armed came
And laid their hands on Jesus
And held Him fast.

A VOICE

As for Him, He's going to die!   There'll be no more kind deeds, or tender
Words that pour upon our burning wounds the music of His power.

ANOTHER VOICE

Scarcely will the distant, far too distant echo of the parables
Brand our sins with an uncertain odour of apples that are sour.

THIRD VOICE

As for Him, He's going to die!   No more Samaritans, sweet spell
That distils the Azure in the cooling fountain and the well.

CHORUS

May shame and dishonour fall upon you, on your sons and race!
May your entrails burn and slowly calcinate in the depth of Hell !
May the serpents and the toads and jackals leave their mark behind
In your execrable bodies rife with leprosy and cancer!

May a hooked and ruthless hand, a mouth no greed can satisfy,
Suck your heart before your eyes and torture what you hold so dear!

May each night a raven croak within the wedlock of your bed,
Changing into terror the delights of your ignoble flesh!

Shame, vile traitor, shame upon you, sluttish soul, rapacious face,
Throughout Life and throughout Death and throughout Time and throughout
    Space!

THE EVANGELIST

Behold one of Jesu's disciples stretched out his hand
And flourishing his sword he smote one of the priests'
Attendants, cutting off his ear.
        Then Jesus said :

JESUS

Put back thy sword into its place,
For every one who takes the sword
    Shall perish by the sword.
And dost thou think I cannot now
    Pray to My Father
Who shall send Me in a moment
    Twelve legions of angels ?
How then shall be fulfilled
    The Scriptures ?
    Thus must it be.

THE EVANGELIST

And turning to the crowd He said :

JESUS

Are ye come with swords and staves
To take Me
As ye'd come against a thief ?
Every day
I sat amongst you in the Temple
Yet ye took Me not.
All this was done
In order that the writings
Of the prophets might be fulfilled.

THE EVANGELIST

All the disciples then
Forsook Jesus and fled.

A VOICE

As for Him, He's going to die!   No more Samaritans, sweet spell
That distils the Azure in the cooling fountain and the well.

41

CHORUS

O adulterous woman, Forest, Night and Future, Past and Death,
Tear your veils to pieces, cry, and bow your faces to the earth!
Those eyes nevermore shall see the light that judged your mystery,
The brow bends that pacified your solitary misery.

Mountain, Lake and Valley, sparkling waters of the bitter Sea,
Wring your entrails, let your tears fall, join the Mother with your tears!
Soon the hand will stiffen that once guided sail and lightest barque,
Nailèd soon the feet shall be that charmed both wave and poisonous snake.

Beggars, Lepers, let your tears fall freely as you bite the dust!
He shall perish, He that came and pacified your misery,
He who in each ulcer poured the soothing incense of His heart,
Changing all your wind-worn rotten rags in draperies of light.

Lightning, Thunder, Tempest, Blasphemy, and Doubt, and Malediction,
Shed your tears for Him who often pardoned your vituperation,
Changing all your pointless fears in salutory warning voice
Thus to petrify the tiger and keep Crime in its abode.

Nightingale, and lark, and little children, cry, oh! cry!
For your Father, Brother, Friend, and Babe, to Calvary draws nigh.

PART II

A VOICE

Ah! how strangely that bird its melody has sung :
One would have thought its voice was floundering in the mud,
And that its frantic prayer towards the Azure flung
All pearly with the dawn had fallen with a thud.

Ah! how strangely that waterfall its tears have flung :
One would have thought it mused a wicked god's intent ;
And that its curve, instead of questioning among
The Blue, humbly, defied it with a stern dissent.

Ah! how strangely the branches of that vine have swung :
To mock the harvesting one would have thought it wished
To dip its branches in the waters of the Blue
And hide them 'neath the horrors of a Future Day.

Ah! how strangely that little child its cry has flung :
One would have thought it wished to hail the archangel's zeal
Which set all dreams at nought and darted through the Blue
To swoop upon the evil Dragon, armed with steel.

CHORUS

Tremble, you cold-hearted men, you widows, orphans, cursèd race!
Tremble, Kings and Beggars, Weak and Strong, you Cut-throats and your Victims!
Girt with lightning, leaning o'er us, the chastening God meditates
And seeks a torment terrible enough to punish all our crimes.

A VOICE

I wandered once upon the roofs
Heavy with love and with intent
To live, when, suddenly a star
Made clear to me a ship afar
Which rocked itself upon the sea ;
I understood the bitter sense
Of ' appetite,' of ' constancy,'
Of ' distance,' and ' futurity.'

CHORUS

Tremble, cowardly brows and stinking bodies!   Tremble, Hypocrites,
—Salt of impure kisses 'neath the flatness of unleavened bread—
For the Lamb of God who feels the Cross less heavy than our rites,
Drags in vain both Love and Pardon toward the hill's disastrous head.

A VOICE

I wandered once upon the roofs
Heavy with pain and with intent

To die, when, suddenly a star
Made clear to me a ship afar
Which rocked itself upon the sea ;
I understood the bitter sense
Of words like ' sleep ' and words like ' truce,'
Of words like ' dream,' and ' yesterday,' and ' hitherto.'

CHORUS

All the roofs shall disappear, the sails shall desiccate the sea,
All the stars shall scrutinize another and more bitter gulf.

A VOICE

In vain I searchèd for the roofs,
I sought in vain for the intent
To live ; when, suddenly, a star
Made clear to me a ship afar
Which, tired of waiting on the sea,
Broke up upon the bitter wastes
Where the ravens of Hopefulness
Gnawed at my posthumous distress.

CHORUS

As for Him, He 's going to die!   There'll be no more kind deeds, or tender
Words that pour upon our burning wounds the music of His power.
Scarcely will the distant, far too distant echo of the parables

Brand our sins with an uncertain odour of apples that are sour.
As for Him, He's going to die!   No more Samaritans, sweet spell
That distils the Azure in the cooling fountain and the well.

THE EVANGELIST

And they that had laid hold of Jesus took Him up to the High Priest
Where all the Elders and the Scribes were gathered.   And then all the priests
Took counsel with each other to bear false witness against their Lord,
And find some cause to give Him up to Death.   And Caiaphas spake thus :

CAIAPHAS

Art Thou the Christ, the Son of God ?   I adjure Thee by the living God
To tell us.

THE EVANGELIST

And Jesus answered and said :

JESUS

I am—the Son of Man
Whom ye shall see surrounded by the clouds, sitting on the Father's right.

When Caiaphas heard these words he shouted out :

CAIAPHAS
                              What blasphemy!
And now what further need have we of any better witnesses,
For ye yourselves just now have heard Him speak.   'Tis He.
                              What do ye think ?

THE PHARISEES

He is guilty
Of death!

THE EVANGELIST

*And thereupon
They struck Jesus,
Spat in His face
And said to Him :*

THE PHARISEES

Thou art the Christ,
Yet dost Thou know
Who smote Thee ?

CHORUS

He knew it, and we knew it too!   And the whole Earth
Knew it, the Sea knew it, and also every Star.
The powers of Darkness knew it too and so did Light,
And Hell's inferno knew it, inexorable brutes!

The punishment awaiting you is better far
Than all the punishments you have to suffer here :
Upon the Day of Judgment the celestial Wrath
Shall make your hardened hearts to melt in many a tear.

Ah! you shaii see them then—you'll see them for all time!
The vile abyss fashioned by your indignity
And the pathetic scorn of the features sublime ;

And when you shall have reckoned up your heavy crime
And when you've cried for the Victim's extremity
In vain your tears shall flow during eternity!

THE EVANGELIST

A damsel came to Peter as he sat
Within the palace gate and said to him :

FIRST DAMSEL
Thou also wast with Jesus.

THE EVANGELIST
But Peter, taken unawares,
Denied the thing and said :

PETER
I know not what thou sayest.

THE EVANGELIST
And as he was going out
Another damsel came
And said to those that stayed :

SECOND DAMSEL
This fellow was with this Jesus.

THE EVANGELIST
Again Peter denied the thing
And swore upon an oath :

PETER
No! no! I do not know the man!

THE EVANGELIST

And they that stood by said
To him :

THE PHARISEES

        Most certainly
Thou also wast with Him.
Thy speech bewrayeth thee.

THE EVANGELIST

Then he began to swear and said :

PETER

No! no! I do not know the man!

THE EVANGELIST

And immediately the cock began to crow.
Then Peter called to mind the words of Jesus :
'Before the cock crow, thou shalt deny Me thrice.'
      And then
      Going out
      He wept
      Bitterly.

A VOICE

I had a lovely golden bird
That flew away without a word.

I had a very gentle kid
That tumbled down a hidden pit.

I had a faithful dog and dear
Now lying at the bottom of the mere.

I had a lovely white-winged dove
Buried beneath the snow above.

I had a cock that used to cry
Each time my heart would tell a lie.

THE EVANGELIST

As soon as day was come the chief priests and the elders of the people
Took counsel, and having bound Jesus, led away the Master
And delivered Him to Pontius Pilate.

As was wont
The Governor released unto the people at that solemn feast
The prisoner whose chains they wished to be released.
Now as he had a famous prisoner called Barabbas,
 The Chief Priests and the Elders
 Persuaded all the people
 To send Jesus to the gallows
 And to release Barabbas.
 So Pilate said to them :

PILATE

Whom will ye I release ?

THE EVANGELIST

They all replied :

THE PHARISEES
 Barabbas!

THE EVANGELIST

Then Pilate said :

PILATE
 What shall I do
With Jesus called the Christ?

THE EVANGELIST

They all replied :

THE PHARISEES

Let Him be crucified!

THE EVANGELIST

And Pilate said :

PILATE

Why ?
What evil hath He done ?

A VOICE

The blind have seen,
The blind have seen!
The deaf have heard,
The deaf have heard!
The dumb have spoken,
The dumb have spoken!
The old, infirm, and paralytic men have walked!

Lepers are cured,
Lepers are cured!
The poor have laughed,
The poor have laughed!
He promised Heaven
To the children of Israel,
Our dear departed rose in answer to His call!

ANOTHER VOICE

The blind have seen!
The deaf have heard!
The dumb have spoken!
The old, infirm, and paralytic men have walked!
Lepers are cured!
The poor have laughed!
He drove our demons out from us and showed us Heaven,
Our dear departed rose in answer to His call!

THE EVANGELIST

They cried again the more :

THE PHARISEES

Let Him be crucified!   Let Him be crucified!

THE EVANGELIST

Then Pilate, nought availing,
And seeing the tumult grow,
Took water and washed his hands
Before the crowd and said :

PILATE

Of this blood I am innocent.
Do ye do as ye will with Him.

THE EVANGELIST

And all the people cried :

THE PHARISEES

His blood be on our hands
And on our children's hands!

THE EVANGELIST

Then Pilate released Barabbas
And took Jesus and scourged Him
And gave Him up to be crucified.

A VOICE

O stay your hands, ye butchers, stay.   O let Him free!
If ye 'd approach this body, then do so on your knee.

This body that ye'd desecrate with your foul blows
Will smell to-morrow of the cedar and the rose.

These hands and feet through which your cruel nails will beat
Shall make the lilies whiter and the grass more sweet.

Whereas your flesh already savours of the crow,
The wolf and jackal and the stinking sewage flow.

Ah! soon! the terrible judgment hour is soon to be!
Down on your knee! down on your knee! down on your knee!

THE EVANGELIST

Having led Jesus to the common hall,
   The soldiers of the Priest
Stripped Him and dressed Him in a scarlet robe,
   And platted Him a crown of thorns
   And put it on His head,

And at the same time
They put a reed in His right hand.
Then as they bowed the knee before Him
They mocked Him saying :

THE PHARISEES

Hail, King of the Jews!

THE EVANGELIST

And as they spat on Him,
They took the reed
And smote Him on the head.

A VOICE

My whole body breathes narcissus perfume and carnation,
In my golden hair there blooms the message of the rose,
My two eyes perfume all disrespect and tribulation ;
With my breathing I embalm the abysmal sighs of Cause.

Cool, my tears are cool and fresh as any mountain spring ;
Warm and genial are my kisses like a dove's soft wing ;
More sonorous is my voice than echoes following me,
Echoes of a voice lost in the labyrinth of the tombs.

To anoint Thy forehead I remember all the passion
That I learned so long ago in the far distant South
Where the women carry in the lewdness of their mouth
The salt of ocean and the sweetness of the spring.

Tear my body! Munch carnation and narcissus bloom!
Breathe my hair e'en though Thou crush the roses and their message!
Tell me, too, about the anguish and delight of torture,
Odious Effect that makes Cause tremble with dark gloom.

ANOTHER VOICE

Body—narcissi, carnation ;—
Hair—and bloom of rose ;—
Scent of tribulation
And murmur of Cause.

Upon the mountain, plaints—
Kisses of the doves,
And the voice that haunts
Me amongst the tombs ;

Every new caress
Learned in distant lands,
Lips lewd with excess
—Seas, and all the springs. . . .

'Tis for Thee the mountain,
'Tis for Thee the doves,
'Tis for Thee the friend
Searching in the tombs ;

For Thee each caress
Learned in distant lands,
Springs flush with excess :
Seas, and watery wastes.

For Thee the carnations,
Narcissi and rose,
For me all the tribulations—
Both Effect and Cause.

THE EVANGELIST

And having mocked Him thus
They took away the robe
And put His own clothes on
And led Him away to be crucified.
Now, on the way,
They met a man called Simon
And asked him
To carry Jesu's Cross.

When they were come
Unto a place called Golgotha
There they crucified Jesus
Between two thieves,
One on His right,
One on His left.
And they that passed by cursed Him
And shook their head
And said :

THE PHARISEES

Now save Thyself,
Thou that destroyest the Temple, and in three days
Rebuildest it.
Art Thou the Son of God ?
Then come down from the Cross!

THE EVANGELIST

The Chief Priests, and the Elders, and the Scribes cried out :
'He saved others, but Himself He cannot save !
If He be King of Israel let Him come down
And we'll believe in Him.'
The thieves beside Him crucified
Insulted Him in the same way.

A VOICE

To anoint Thy forehead I remember all the passion
That I learned so long ago in the far distant South
Where the women carry in the lewdness of their mouth
The salt of ocean and the sweetness of the spring.

ANOTHER VOICE

Ah! that day when Thy raiment white
Went rustling by my prison wall
I rushed towards the mystic sight
Like one whose madness hears the call.

Ah! listen! that magnetic voice
That prophesied healing repose,
That made with stars the hearth rejoice
And filled the horizon with a rose.

That hair! its colour and its form
That calmed the murmur and the storm
Of Discontent, the stifling dread

Of Hell! Ah! those hands' ivory
That crowned with power and victory
The little children's tender head!

THE EVANGELIST

Now from the sixth hour
There was darkness over all the land
Until the ninth hour.
About the ninth hour
With a loud voice
Jesus said :

JESUS

Eli, Eli, lama Sabachthani.

THE EVANGELIST

That is to say :
My God, My God,
Why hast Thou forsaken Me ?

A VOICE

My soul is sad even unto death.
A thousand vipers rob my breath.
Indifferent, the whole earth sleeps.
The golden-voiced lovers dream
Of their delight, of their remorse,
And greedy man tells out his gold.
My soul is sad even unto death.

64

CHORUS

Over Thy body and Thy soul be lord,
Thy Father holds the true reward.
Quietens the sea, the wind 's no breath,
Beneath Thy feet is groaning Death.
List to the Azure's golden breath!

THE EVANGELIST

Some of them that stood there
Said when they heard that :

THE PHARISEES

This man calleth
For Elias.

THE EVANGELIST

And one of them
Ran, and took a sponge,
And dipped it in vinegar,
And having fixed it
On a reed

E

Gave it to Him
  To drink.
But others said :

THE PHARISEES

Let be, and let us see
If Elias will come to save Him.

THE EVANGELIST

Jesus cried again
  With a loud voice
And yielded up the ghost.

A VOICE

O bring me roses, bring me lilies—bring me many roses
And many lilies,—jasmin and the little marguerites,
Carnations of a crimson colour, carnations pink and yellow,
And many, especially, of my belovèd violets,

Of those so chaste in bloom they still seem in their tender years,
Which fear the waters, fear the breeze and the bees of Sybaris,
The sunshine of the Apotheosis with its burning rays,
The clamorous dejections and the hypocritic tears.

THE EVANGELIST

And, lo ! the veil of the temple
  Was rent in twain,
From top to bottom
  And the earth shook,
And the rocks were rent asunder
And the graves were disembowelled ;
And several bodies of the Saints which slept
  Arose,
  And stepping from their graves
  They came into the Holy City
  . And many saw them.
    Then the centurion
  And those that were with him
    Watching Jesus
Saw the earth quake
And those things that were done,
  And seized with fright
    They cried :
'Truly this was the Son of God !'
  Now there were present
A far way off several women
Who had followed Jesus from Galilee,
  Ministering unto Him.

Amongst them were
Mary Magdalene,
Mary the mother of James and Joses,
And the mother of the sons of Zebedee.
When even came
A rich man out of Arimathaea,
Naméd Joseph,
A disciple of Jesus,
Went to Pilate
And begged the body of Jesus.
And Pilate commanded the body to be delivered.

A VOICE

Cool, my tears are cool and fresh as any mountain spring ;
Warm and genial are my kisses like a dove's soft wing ;
More sonorous is my voice than echoes following me,
Echoes of a voice lost in the labyrinth of the tombs.

ANOTHER VOICE

O bring me roses, bring me lilies—bring me many roses
And many lilies,—jasmin and the little marguerites,
Carnations of a crimson colour, carnations pink and yellow,
And many, especially, of my belovèd violets,

Of those so chaste in bloom they still seem in their tender years,
Which fear the waters, fear the breeze and the bees of Sybaris,
The sunshine of the Apotheosis with its burning rays,
The clamorous dejections and the hypocritic tears.

THE EVANGELIST

And Joseph took the body,
And wrapped it in a linen cloth
And laid it in his own new tomb
Which he had hewn out of the rock.
Then he rolled
A great stone to the entrance of the tomb
And went away.
Mary Magdalene
And the other Mary
Were sitting there
Over against the sepulchre.

A VOICE

List to the Azure's golden breath!

CHORUS

Good night, belovèd Jesus, Jesus mine, good night!

A VOICE

Quietens the sea, the wind's no breath.

CHORUS

Good night, belovèd Jesus, Jesus mine, good night!

A VOICE

My body's crying out for death.

CHORUS

Good night, belovèd Jesus, Jesus mine, good night!

A VOICE

My soul is sad even unto death.

CHORUS

Good night, belovèd Jesus, Jesus mine, good night!

GRAND CHORUS

Good night, belovèd Jesus, Jesus mine, good night!
All children—all Thy children, shall guard Thee through the night

In the Heaven of Thy Father there's no star in sight :
Good night, belovèd Jesus, Jesus mine, good night!

Let there be none who shall to tears or noise incite.
Good night, belovèd Jesus, Jesus mine, good night!

O'er the ruins of the Temple no bird sings to-night.
Good night, belovèd Jesus, Jesus mine, good night!

Good night, belovèd Jesus, Jesus mine, good night!
The children and the birds shall guard Thee in the night.

The sea is motionless, the horizon fades from sight.
Good night, belovèd Jesus, Jesus mine, good night!

Good night, belovèd Jesus, Jesus mine, good night!
Thou'lt heal our flagging souls with the promise of Thy light.

With myrrh the children's dreams shall perfume Thy dark night.
Good night, belovèd Jesus, Jesus mine, good night!

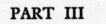

PART III

**Sinite
parvulos
venire
ad me**

THE PHARISEES

Come to life again, come now! sinister bard of misery,
Friend of every vagabond and worker of iniquity!
Come back as 'tis written, armèd with the Sceptre of Thy Father!
Hear our cry, we whom Thou often call'dst the Temple's common trader.

Ah! come if Thou dare! For Thou shalt climb anew Thy Calvary,
Ridiculed by that same multitude which contemplates Thy shroud,
Fearing nothing, in its knowledge that the justice of the people
Triumphed when it imprisoned Thee in a tomb fit for the common crowd.

Henceforth Thou shalt lie, the butt and execration of wise men
Whose power and whose riches Thou wast keen to give away to robbers
Through that crazy dream of Thine to build a palace in the clouds,

There to lodge all Cowardice, all Recklessness and Laziness.
Nay! we do not fear Archangels, neither do we fear Thy Father!
Come back, then, O charlatan, sinister bard of misery!

JESUS

. . . .

. . . .

THE DEAD

Rise up again! Come dance with us the necrologic dance
Which we dance every night upon the pathway of the tombs.
The stars will fade away : the curvèd moon—beak or poniard—
Makes them turn pale.   May Thine abundant love protect these doves!

O guide us with Thine eyes! No Will o' the wisp, no heavenly orb
Can e'er compare with Thy pure countenance that looketh down
From high—much higher than the countenance of unctuous gods
Whose haughty power was fond of Splendour and of Hecatombs.

Henceforth it is Thine unobtrusiveness shall lead our dance.
With our limbs rendered supple we shall mark the tender rhythm
Of every sympathetic souvenir that we have cherished,

Instead of stirring up the wretched torment of our envy
Beleaguered by the strident chords of atrabilious Death
Who sleeps, dead also, near Thy Cross, upon the Calvary.

JESUS

. . . .

. . . .

THE NIGHT

I have need of Thee, I need to breathe in through Thy hair
The perfume that finds its way through walls and through remorse,
And to smell the balm, the elixir, and the great flame
Of Thine eyes that scrutinize the black pit of my bowels.

I have need of Thee so that Thy word may qualify
Every timid dream the children dream, so that Thou mock
Him who can but think of puffing out his vanity,
Dreaming of the pomp and circumstance of his own burial.

I have need of Thee!   Come, lie beneath my welcome shade.
Rest Thy forehead on the silence of my silver glade.
Plunge Thy heavy sighings in the sobbings of my springs.

From my humblest little bird to the uncharted stars,
All my crimes, my sorrows, and my loves, all, all accord
To request again the shelter of Thy gentle word.

JESUS

. . . .

. . . .

F

THE NIGHTINGALE

Come back, Jesus! Come back and listen to my praise,
The melodious canticle of my ingenuous love.
I'll sing to Thee much better than the Angels do.
I'll sing my roundels for Thee through the nights and days.

The Angels' song is soothing like the song of wrens,
But their heart beats too quickly and their breath is short,
Whereas when I sing, I can lengthen my strange lays
And make them modulate or make them tedious too.

A little while ago I found a novel song
To celebrate the joy of the immortal news,
For I am sure to-morrow Thou'lt come near the well.

Ah! since Thou canst change everything, ah! do Thou cause,
To hasten my delight, the rosy-fingered dawn
To lead Thy steps to us in the middle of the night.

JESUS

. . . .

. . . .

THE LARK

Come!   Sustain this lyric voice that celebrates
Opening day, apotheosis of Thy Glory,
And which drives away the last funereal shade
Veiling in the depth of Heaven Thine ivory brow.

Those two mountains rendered famous by Thy torment
Tremble 'neath the premonition of my song,
For 'tis I who, modulating in the shade,
Prophesied to Thee the victory's aftermath.

Here it is.   Here is the Kingdom of Thy Father
In its early days.   O Thou who makest gather
In my tiny throat the glory of Thy light,

Come, grant with Thine eyes the dream I treasure most!
May the music of my song for ever live!
And may twilight never supersede this dawn!

JESUS

. . . .

. . . .

A BLIND MAN

I see the iris of Thy warm regard
That breaks the back of Time and Death and Crime
And overthrows the Hydra and the Guard,
The chillèd sun and heavy reeling night.

I see the lightning and the eternal flames,
The flight of condors and doves in pursuit,
And, 'neath the arbour and the doorway frames,
Masses of spikenard and buttercups.

I see the Future with Thy open doors
For feeble bodies and for virile souls,
For those in poverty who shall be kings.

Come, touch mine eyes and let me see myself
In Thee, clothèd in purple and with myrrh,
Son, Father, Holy Ghost, God, Three in One!

JESUS

. . . .

. . . .

THE LIGHTNING

I am tired of terrorizing sinners,
Tired of rousing profitless remorse,
Tired of scanning the great waste of fields,
Tired of disturbing the reptile's sleep.

I am tired of flashing over songs
Voiced by threatening mouths of subtle seers,
Tired of hastening the alluring gifts
Of the pious 'neath the peristyles.

I am tired of shining on the hand
Of a vain god whose inhuman heart
Turns us into signals of distress.

Come! Much better than a Jove Thou canst
Steer my quivering light across the Sky
Towards the undying fervour of Thy stars.

JESUS

. . . .

. . . .

THE THUNDERBOLT

I wait Thine order to come down
And carbonize Thine enemies
Instead of the tender mournful tree
That 's filled with nests and plaintiveness.

Ah! could I see the Emperors' pride,
Their bones, their granite, and their bronze
A-dancing in the wind with the ashes
Of many an unpunished crime!

O lift Thine omni-puissant hand
And put Thy finger on my catch.
Already I know the tainted land :

The castle hold, the hidden watch,
The vipers' barricaded tree
That on this Cross have nailèd Thee.

JESUS

. . . .

. . . .

A BEGGAR

Every one would turn me out.
Yet am I in no man's way :
I am simply waiting here
Till Thou rise again, till ring

The promised hour.   Shivering
With cold, I await Thy voice
Gently calling to me : ' Lo!
Take thy sword and take thy crown.'

And I promise to be proud,
Yet not too proud—generous
With each call that is sincere.

Come! I cannot bear it longer!
Dost Thou know I fear to die
Ere I've won my victory!

JESUS

. . . .

. . . .

THE MOUNTAIN

Return and sit with me
Beside the slender grass
Which sways in the evening breeze
The echo of Thy words.

My summit is the censer
Wherein Thy Symbols smoke.
The stars shall fall therein
To win Thy sympathy.

My waters harbour sighs
For every penitent.
My grass is full of fragrance

For every new distress.
My goats have lovely eyes
Alight with sympathies.

JESUS

. . . .

. . . .

A LEPER

Hasten Thy return!
I am dead with shame!
Come before the dawn!
Listen while I tell

Of the fatal love
Which is conquering me.
For it's like a vulture
Soaring, ever soaring

From my leprous feet
To my bruisèd eyes
Watching for my Love.

Come and cure me, come!
I feel that my faith
Weakens with her love.

JESUS

. . . .

. . . .

THE FOREST

Dawn's rival sign—
Thy noble eyes
Shall bring to flower
My eglantine,

And fill with sound
My chestnut trees,
My sycomores
And coccagees.

At Thy command
My fire-flies bright
Shall fly away

To deck with wings
And sparkling light
Thy noble brow.

JESUS

. . . .

. . . .

JUDAS

O the torture
Of my bed!
For remorse
Grips my head,

Pricks my body
As with gorse
And gnaws
At my belly.

Come!   Thine arms!
Thou shalt come
—Thou it is!—

Bringing bliss
With a kiss
From Thy lips.

JESUS

. . . .

. . . .

THE FLOWERS

O come and cull,
But take us not!
O come and smell
And hear our lot.

Why shouldst Thou bruise
The tender stem ?
For 'tis its muse
That gave us life.

Thou knowest well—
Under Thy spell
Were born these doves

Whose eye so soft
Watches aloft
Upon the roofs.

JESUS

. . . .

. . . .

THE SEA

Thy closed eyes consume
My heart's beat that raves.
Light upon my spume!
Walk upon my waves!

Calm the bitterness
Of my long complaints,
The posthumous distress
Of my sea-born saints.

In my dark resounding
Bosom there 's no dawn
Smiles at their awaking.

Come!   O touch my waves!
And my ocean graves
Shall behold the morn.

JESUS

. . . .
. . . .

THE PAST

O come and wash my sins,
The crimes of all my kings,
My feet all worn and torn
While carrying my cross.

I've ridden far across
The Night and its alarms,
I've walked and walked and walked
Around the chilly abyss.

Give me, O give me light!
Scatter my dust abroad
And let the four winds blow!

Then lead me on the road
Where feedeth Innocence
Beneath the moving reeds.

JESUS

. . . .

. . . .

THE FUTURE

Touch my brow that they may know
Thou gav'st me the breath of life,
And that my head bears the plumes
Of Rejoicing and of Love.

May my enterprising flight
Never find the air too heavy ;
And remind me of my fight
At each new perplexity.

Keep me far from the believers,
Those who try to classify
Truth and Hope and Charity.

Conquest! Empire! Hear'st Thou not ?
Come! before Thy martyrdom
Tempt the conquerors' restraint.

JESUS

. . . .

. . . .

CHORUS OF YOUNG MAIDENS

Seeing Thy calm sad countenance,
Thine arms whiter than any swan's,
We chose Thee for our husband, once,
When Thou wast praying near the vines.

Come, tell us which among us, please,
Is noblest and the worthiest
Of lauding Thee upon her knees,
Of witnessing the double zest

Of Thine own love and of the love
Of the poor whose burden is so heavy
For souls both weak and frivolous ;

Thy burden shall be light for us,
O Shepherd, since we call ourselves
The sheep of Thine own parables.

JESUS

. . . .

. . . .

SATAN

Come back, then!   O come down here again!
Lay the foundation of the Father's Realm!
Thou shalt find the people are so vain,
Basely choosing the viper for the lamb.

Barabbas, not Jesus, is their choice,
Ribaldry, not Love.   And they disdain . . .
Ah! if Thou wouldst rule them with Thy voice,
Peaceably, just think what they would gain! . . .

It were better to be Four than Three.
Splendid 'tis to die upon the Cross,
But the conquest must not lose its gloss.

To undermine the Christian edifice—
Nothing, just a murmur will suffice :
Let the Devil smile—that will suffice.

JESUS

. . . .

. . . .

DEATH

Away!   Every caress is known to me.
There 's too much lenience in Thine ivory hands
And in Thy kisses too much sympathy
Which Thy transcending eye has won from Heaven.

Thou cam'st down here to pour Thine ecstasy
Upon the sheenless brows of my dear Dead,
And when Thou sleepest Thy sleep oppresses me
And when I see Thou art dead, myself I die!

'Tis said that at to-morrow's dawn the sea
Shall vibrate in Thy deep resounding heart.
Well then, come back to life!   Away!   Arise!

Thy dream is far too full of melodies,
Thy Will o' the wisp is a devouring fire,
Thy sacred heavy body makes me tire.

JESUS

. . . .

. . . .

THE WOMAN OF SAMARIA

I've been waiting for Thee by this well since dawn.
Come while my amphora's water is still fresh.
Thou knowest 'tis the same amphora, the same well
That Thou sawest one summer day, with parchèd throat,

And Thy heart brimming with love, that heart which gilds
Every sunset, every dawn and every peach,
Which the sick cry unto and the eagle, blind,
Craves, as groping wild it flees the arrow's reach.

I've been waiting for Thee by this well whose sighs
Have a longing to be poured upon Thy wounds,
And accompany Thy sad consoling guise.

Thou shalt come!   E'en now I feel my heart on fire.
Ah yes! I shall see the stars shine in Thine eyes
And at Thy word every prejudice expire.

JESUS

. . . .

. . . .

THE DISCIPLES

Lord, Lord, the work of love has scarcely yet begun.
To finish it would be a Herculean feat.
We want a miracle—the last Thou shalt perform—
To subjugate Future and Present at Thy feet.

That tragic memorable evening when at Supper
Thou didst foretell by which one Thou wouldst be betrayed,
Didst not Thou pass around to us the loving cup
And promise that one day we'd drink the precious wine

With Thee when Thou hadst reached the Kingdom of Thy Father?
Oh! tell us! Didst Thou mean by this that Thy Apostles
Should follow Thee until they reach the Valley of Death?

Oh! speak! For we are ready. Speak! Our heart is strong.
If Thou shouldst see it quake, or should we lose our breath,
Thou'lt know we cannot bear the gospel burden farther.

JESUS

. . . .

. . . .

THE THREE KINGS

Unto Thee we come directed by that self-same star
Which the light feet of the dromedaries followed once.
Come! For here is incense, myrrh, and gold. Lift up the dismal
Veil which now is covering the wounds of Calvary.

Everywhere we're told the sky is veilèd with Thy death,
But we find it all pervaded both with hope and light.
Ah! look!—over there!—how quickly he descends with wings,
Gabriel the Angel! See Thy Mother's countenance!

For She's understood. Her happiness begins again.
Once more She shall call to mind the sweet joys of Thy birth,
Her ecstatic passion, her caresses . . . and Thy smile!

And Thine open arms and Her expectant virtuous hands ;
Here once more the shepherds are, the good sheep of their flocks,
Here once more is incense, here is gold, and here is myrrh!

JESUS

. . . .

. . . .

MARY MAGDALENE

Oh come! oh come and touch me! for they say I am insane
Because, a little while ago, I saw Thee standing up
Like Lazarus ; I heard Thy steps, I heard Thy breath and voice
And saw Thee look at me, that look which barbarous Death had veiled.

Yes, I have seen Thee.   Clothed in white, a halo round Thy brow,
With lilies gathered in Thy hands, wrapped in Thy flowing robe,
Thou spak'st, and as the words fell from Thy lips, each flower, each crown
Leaned over like a bridge that spans the infinite abyss.

Oh come!   Oh come!   Give me Thy look.   For the last time console
—And afterwards Thou canst go up into Thy Realm of Light—
This love, this hopeless love which eats into my very bosom,

Which fills up the abysmal pit and overthrows the walls.
Oh lay Thy hands upon these people who said I was insane,
But keep for me alone Thy word and the light in Thine eyes!

JESUS

. . . .

. . . .

MARY

Come! Come! Come! Oh come! my son, my lamb, Master and cherubin
Ah! Thy hands, Thy tiny hands so pink, Thy countenance, Thy smile!
The inexorable seven daggers which empierce my side
Shall, at Thy voice, turn to kisses soft as muted violin.

I have only just begun to love Thee, and to know Thee well,
That day when the shades of Heaven made clear to me Thy martyrdom.
At Thy feet I fall prostrate and humbly beg that Thou shalt guide
My great love, far greater than the love this azure sky can tell.

The inexorable seven daggers which empierced my side
Have become already kisses soft as muted violin.
I have only just begun to love Thee, and to know Thee well,

That day when my heart's alarm made clear to me Thy martyrdom.
Come! Come! Come! Oh come! my son, my lamb, Master and cherubin!
Lay Thy smile upon my hands and lay Thy hands upon my smile.

JESUS

. . . .

. . . .

A LITTLE CHILD

Jesus, little Jesus, I'm so very tired.   All my limbs ache.
May I go to sleep and feel sure that I'll see Thee when I wake?
Is it true that Thou wilt rise again?   Or is there some mistake?

JESUS

Yes, yes, thou mayst go to sleep.   I shall rise again for thy sake.

FINIS

BIBLIOGRAPHY

By Armand Godoy

A José-Maria de Heredia (Lemerre), 1925.

Triste et Tendre.   Préface de Jean Royère (Emile-Paul Frères), 1927.

Le Carnaval de Schumann.   Préface de Camille Mauclair (Emile-Paul Frères), 1927.

Caméléon, en société avec Francis de Miomandre (Emile-Paul Frères), 1927.

Hosanna sur le Sistre (Emile-Paul Frères), 1927.

Monologue de la Tristesse et Colloque de la Joie (Emile-Paul Frères), 1928.

Le Drame de la Passion (Emile-Paul Frères), 1929.

Foch (Emile-Paul Frères), 1929.

Le Corbeau d'Edgar Poe, traduction en vers (Emile-Paul Frères), 1930.

Poèmes Choisis de José Marti, traduction en vers (Emile-Paul Frères), 1930.

Le Brasier Mystique (Emile-Paul Frères), 1930.

Quatre Nocturnes, traduction en vers (Emile-Paul Frères), 1930.

Les Litanies de la Vierge (Albert Messein), 1930.

Le Poème de l'Atlantique (Emile-Paul Frères), 1931.

Les Petits Souliers Roses de Jose Marti, traduction en vers (Emile-Paul Frères), 1931.

Marcel (Emile-Paul Frères), 1932.

Ite Missa Est (Grasset), 1933.

Du Cantique des Cantiques au Chemin de la Croix (Grasset), 1934.

Translations

Paginas Escogidas.   Traduzione di Eduardo Aviles Ramirez.   Prefazione di Jean Royère (Editions Excelsior), 1929.

Le Litanie della Virgine cantate in siciliano da V. De Simone.   (Siculorum Gymnasium, Milano, 1931.)

La Ninna Nanna de Gesù Christe. Adattamento in dialetto pugliese della terza parte de ' Le Drame de la Passion.' (Casa Editrice Aretusa, Milano, 1932.)

Le Litanias de la Virgen. Traduzione e prefazione spagnuola di E. Aviles Ramirez. Madrid, Mèson de Panos, 8, 1932.

Ite Missa Est. Traduzione italiana di Aldi Rizzi. (Editore Ghirlanda, Milano, 1935.)

Il Dramma della Passione. Versione Poetica di Salvatore Lo Presti. (Siculorum Gymnasium, Milano, 1935.)

Dal Cantico Dei Cantici Alla via della Croce. Versione poetica italiana di Vincenzo De Simone. (Siculorum Gymnasium, Milano, 1935.)

BOOKS OF REFERENCE

Hommage à Armand Godoy. (Mediterranea, mars 1929.)

Quelques réflexions sur Armand Godoy à propos du Drame de la Passion, par Francis de Miomandre. (Govone, 1930.)

Armand Godoy, par André Devaux. (Editions des Portiques, 1933.)

Le Musicisme, par Jean Royère. (Messein, 1929.)

Armando Godoy, poeta frances. Carlos Martins. (Editorial Ercilla, Santiago, 1935.)

Armand Godoy. A. Jàcono. (Edizioni latine, Milano, 1935.)

BY MALCOLM McLAREN

Poems, Théo Varlet. Verse translations. (The Village Press, Idbury, Oxon.)

Douze sonnets et un poème, Théo Varlet. Text and translation in facsimile autograph. (Mercure de Flandre. Obtainable from Hachette, London.)

Anthologie de la Poésie Française. Les Modernes. Préface du Professor E. Rudler. (Hachette, London.)

Poèmes. Préface de Théo Varlet. (Mercure de Flandre. From Hachette, London.)

PRINTED IN GREAT BRITAIN BY
A. R. MOWBRAY & CO. LIMITED, LONDON AND OXFORD